W9-BMD-330

PLAYOFFS

NBA

NBA
PLAYOFFS

UNITED CENTER

CHICAGO BULLS

NBA

To Vicki, whose intelligence, coupled with desire, strength, and the ability to work above and beyond human endurance, while creating an original and exciting design scenario, I openly extend my gratitude and deep love. Without you, there would never have been *The Soul of Michael Jordan and Company*.

In loving memory: To my mother, Frances Sprayregen (1907–1996), whose combination of gentleness, beauty, and wisdom will be with me forever.

In memory of Roger Selby (1933–1995), former director of the Boca Museum of Art, a true friend and a man too gentle to walk among wolves.

Our sincere appreciation to the following individuals and organizations: The Basketball Hall of Fame Library and Public Relations Department; Paul Chung, Paul Chung Literary Agency; Nicholas Granat; David Karmin; Rick Olshak, Orlando Magic Public Relations Department; Peter Pliteris, Nikon Electronic Imaging; Tony Sclafani, Romantic Travel; Peter Sorenson; our editors at Gramercy Books/Random House Value Publishing; Mel Cowher, R. R. Donnelley & Sons; and Eric Weissman.

Grateful acknowledgment is given to the following sources for a number of the short quotes in this book: *Michael Jordan* (Basketball Legends) by Sean Dolan; *The Jordan Rules* by Sam Smith; *Scottie Pippen* by Fred McMane; *Jordan* by Mitchell Krugel; *Bull Session* by Johnny Kerr and Terry Pluto; *Hang Time* by Bob Greene; *Sacred Hoops* by Phil Jackson; *Bull Run!* by Roland Lazenby; *Second Coming* by Sam Smith; *Bad as I Wanna Be* by Dennis Rodman; *Who's Running the Asylum?* by Wilt Chamberlain; and *Sports Illustrated*, *Esquire*, and *Slam* magazines.

Special thanks to: Robin Deutsch, public relations director of the Basketball Hall of Fame, for his belief in this project; Marilyn and Joel Sprayregen, for their loving support and generosity; our dearest "soul mate," Bill Hallberg, for his tutelage, continued support, enthusiasm, and caring. Thanks also to all those who offered their thoughtful comments on our book, including Chuck De Luca, Nikon Electronic Imaging; Connie ("The Hawk") Hawkins; Rick Wester, Christie's; Brooks Johnson, the Chrysler Museum; James Clearwater; and Mark Serota.

Finally, our warm appreciation is extended to Dr. Jack Ramsay, the "Dean of Basketball," for his kind words in the foreword to this book.

The Soul of Michael Jordan and Company

In the photographic style of

Gerald Sprayregen

Foreword by

Dr. Jack Ramsay

Design by

Vicki Sylvester

GRAMERCY BOOKS

New York

This 1998 edition is published by Gramercy Books,™
an imprint of Random House Value Publishing, Inc.,
201 East 50th Street, New York, New York 10022.

Gramercy Books™ and design are trademarks of
Random House Value Publishing, Inc.

Random House
New York • Toronto • London • Sydney • Auckland
http://www.randomhouse.com/

Printed in the United States of America. Bound in Mexico.

The Soul of Michael Jordan and Company is not a publication authorized by
Michael Jordan, the Chicago Bulls, or their representatives or related enterprises.

A CIP catalog record for this book is available from the Library of Congress.

ISBN 0-517-20455-X

8 7 6 5 4 3 2 1

I'm not sure when it all began, my love affair with basketball. When I was growing up during the 1940s, baseball was the dominant sport in America, and partially because of that, stickball was a way of life with all of us Bronx boys. This all changed in 1948, when my family moved to Manhattan, which brought us infinitely closer to Madison Square Garden and the struggling New York Knicks. It's easy to admire winning teams, but your heart and soul cries out in longing for the losers, and this longing eventually turns to love. The accessibility of six concrete courts with steel backboards, iron rims with nets of iron mesh, five minutes from our apartment, romantically nestled in that classic oasis known as Central Park, essentially sealed my passion for the game. I clearly remember my twin brother and I, while in high school, running to "our" courts after a snowfall in mid-January, with our basketball, broom, and shovel. After we had finished cleaning the courts, if no one else came out, we would play "one on one," "horse," or invent new games. Then, hours later, we would trek back home, dragging our shovel and broom against the snow and pavement, exhausted, but filled with dreams of tomorrow's games and conquests. My basketball skills were good enough for a very small high school team, fraternity teams in college, and pick-up three-on-three games for the next fifty years, but basketball scholarships and fat contracts were never thrust in my direction.

I think back thirty years, when I brought my son, Nicholas, to his first NBA game, and the thrill I derived watching him take up 30 percent of his seat, and then trying to explain this fast-moving, high-flying game to a six-year-old. Recently, I took Nicholas' five-year-old son, Matthew, already a basketball legend in his own league, to an NBA game, and watched him cheer every basket his team scored, and moan at each of their turnovers.

Matthew and his cousin, Jesse, along with millions of others young and old throughout the world, are incurable fans of Michael Jordan. The Jordan phenomenon is universal: they proudly wear his jersey, number 23, everywhere . . . to all sporting events, to the movies, to work, on airplanes, and at rock concerts. It crosses all boundaries of color, creed, and social upbringing. Without a question, they buy MJ's endorsements, gulping down Gatorade, rushing to buy Nike's latest Air Jordans, and even wearing Hanes underwear . . . so they can be like Mike. A recent *Fortune* article estimated that Michael Jordan has accounted for putting approximately $10 billion into the gross national product, during his career.

I have been extremely fortunate to have watched hundreds of Chicago Bulls NBA games. I have scoured numerous libraries in three states, and spent a few days doing research at the Basketball Hall of Fame, reading and analyzing the voluminous literature on MJ, but words can't quite capture the man. Photography seems to be the only way to present the nuances of this complex and unique individual. With my camera I have attempted to create something more than a documentary of what is. I try to interpret what I see and, more importantly, what I feel. I take what I can use, shape it, flavor in the excitement, the strength, motion, and speed, and then return it to you, the viewer, hoping that the poetry that I have endeavored to create touches a fiber of commonality with you. Enjoy the journey.

Gerald Sprayregen

T his book is not about championships, but for the record, Michael Jordan has six NBA rings, two Olympic Gold Medals, and played on an NCAA championship team at the University of North Carolina. It's not about statistics either, although Michael has the highest per-game scoring average of any NBA player (31.7) and has led the league in scoring ten times. This book is a special photographic essay and inspiring tribute to a singular athlete captured in some of the most provocative and illuminating images ever taken, from angles and vantage points that make it vastly different from prior books about Michael Jordan and from those surely to follow.

In its purest art form, this book is about the greatest basketball player to ever step on the court and perhaps the most popular athlete in the history of sport. He is captured here in both image and words in ways that will help fans feel more in touch with the very essence of MJ. There are those who say that Mohammed Ali remains the most recognizable athlete in the world, but in my travels around the globe, Michael Jordan is unquestionably the most beloved, admired, and imitated athlete in history. Everyone wants to be like Mike; youngsters wear his number 23 Chicago Bulls jersey on playground courts throughout the world, aspiring players shave their heads in homage, and some wag their tongues when driving to the hoop. Everyone sees him from a personal perspective. That';s where the images of Michael captured from the camera of Gerald Sprayregen take Jordan watchers on an exciting and rewarding trip.

There is only one Michael Jordan . . . and there will never be another quite like him. He's truly one-in-a-million, an opinion I state with confidence. It comes from watching his countless awesome performances on the court, as well as observing his unique ability to handle his off-the-court celebrity with warmth, dignity and charm.

Of all the players I have ever coached or watched perform in my more than fifty years of basketball, I have never seen a player with a will to win like Michael Jordan's. Every time he steps onto the basketball court—and it doesn't matter whether it's against the weakest or the strongest NBA teams; at practice or at a pick-up game in Chapel Hill, North Carolina; or with former Tar Heel teammates—Michael wants to prove he's the best every time he laces up his sneakers. And he does it over and over again.

The majestic photography found in *The Soul of Michael Jordan and Company* portrays the very soul of Michael Jordan and his exceptional passion for basketball. It catches Jordan with his teammates and coaches during the arduous NBA season. These images provide wonderful flavor to the greatest game in the world.

This book depicts Michael Jordan's fierce desire to win. It showcases his speed, his power, his grace, his ability to control the moment. Michael makes things happen. The book clearly gives the reader a feel for Jordan's commanding power and presence on the floor. As a competitor, Michael stands by himself, a notch above all the other great legends of the game already enshrined in the Basketball Hall of Fame. *The Soul of Michael Jordan and Company* also conveys his physical strength and fitness. As a longtime triathlete myself, I truly appreciate Michael's dedication to conditioning. He's a superbly trained athlete—a rare combination of strength, flexibility, agility, and stamina—and since his return from baseball, he has not missed a single practice or game. He usually works out for an hour with his personal trainer before a team practice. That sends a message to his teammates: Be prepared and be in top condition.

There are several photographs that allow glimpses of the inner Jordan—a smile, a wink, or even a laugh from Michael. Along with being the ultimate competitor, he's one of the most generous, kind, and warm-hearted people I've ever met. Everyone wants to be like Mike.

I've been asked often whether the NBA will survive and continue to prosper as Michael Jordan finally hangs up his famous number 23 Chicago Bulls jersey. I am always quick to respond that the league has prospered in the post-Russell, -Chamberlain, -Robertson, -West, -Dr. J, -Magic, and -Bird eras, and so shall it thrive post–Michael Jordan, but it won't be quite the same.

The nice thing about *The Soul of Michael Jordan and Company* is that it's a forever keepsake that will keep Michael alive in our hearts and thoughts for many, many years to come. The book portrays images of Jordan that will remain forever.

Enjoy the poetry in motion.

Dr. Jack Ramsay
Basketball Hall of Famer

There is no way to describe
the sound in the stadium.
You could hear three words:
From North Carolina . . .
Then you could hear only raw,
shuddering noise.
"I've never heard a word
after 'Carolina' . . .
It gives me chills, every time.
You hope people respect you,
but for that immediate moment
you know that they do. . . .
I can't see very much
in the darkness,
but I think they're standing up.
The sense of respect that I get
from the people . . .
I get chill bumps.
Sometimes I'm misty-eyed."

Bob Greene and Michael Jordan

Now this is the Law of the Jungle,

as old and as true as the sky;

And the Wolf that shall keep it may

prosper,

but the Wolf that shall break it must

die.

As the creeper that girdles the tree

trunk,

the Law runneth forward and back.

For the strength of the Pack is the Wolf,

and the strength of the Wolf is the Pack.

Rudyard Kipling
Quote from THE SECOND
JUNGLE BOOK,
often read by Phil Jackson to the Bulls
during the playoffs

Us against the world.

Michael Jordan

It's not easy to juggle the egos of a **Jordan**, a **Pippin,** or a **Rodman.** There are only 240 collective player minutes in every regulation **NBA** game, and each player wants more time on the floor than can be allowed. We review playbacks, we plan, we strategize, but in the end, it's the players who must execute . . . and **sometimes, it's a very long night.**

Gerald Sprayregen

I never would have believed that anyone could score 63 points against us, not in Boston Garden.

But Michael
is the best,
one of a kind.
I've never seen
anyone like him.
Phenomenal . . .
I've never seen
a player have
the impact on
a team that
Michael has had on the Bulls . . .

He is the most awesome player in the NBA. . . .

God played today, and it was Michael Jordan.

Larry Bird, Basketball Hall of Famer

*E*ach year,
Chicago was forced
to reserve a spot on its roster
for a player who would serve
as Jordan's practice fodder—
someone with an ego
strong enough to withstand
the daily humiliation
of going against

the best one-on-one player
in the history of the game. . . .
[He] invariably ended
the season with [his] confidence
shattered, and was seldom
of any use in the league again.

Sean Dolan

SOMETIME IN THE DARK, DISTANT PAST,
THERE MAY HAVE BEEN A BASKETBALL PLAYER
WHO WAS A BETTER CLUTCH SHOOTER THAN **MJ . . .**

BUT I DOUBT IT.

SOMETIME IN THE DARK, DISTANT PAST,
THERE MAY HAVE BEEN A BASKETBALL PLAYER
WHOSE OFFENSIVE AND
DEFENSIVE SKILLS
WERE GREATER THAN **MJ'S . . .**

BUT I DOUBT IT.

HOWEVER, NOT NOW, NOR IN THE DARK, DISTANT PAST,
WAS THERE A BASKETBALL PLAYER
WHO BROUGHT SUCH INTENSITY,
SUCH AN INDOMITABLE NEED TO WIN,
AS **MICHAEL JORDAN** DOES,
EVERY TIME HE STEPS ONTO A COURT.

Gerald Sprayregen

I'm nothing more than a sports slave.

If it's going to be all about money,

We're all being used in this business,

and some guys can sit back and take the trade-off—

Scottie

was the kind of athlete
Krause loves.
He had long arms
and big hands
and the speed
and leaping ability
to become a first-class
all-around player. . . .

Scottie had a near-genius

basketball IQ . . .

and, like Jordan,
seemed to have
a sixth sense
about what was going
to happen next.

Phil Jackson
Former Chicago Bulls Coach

Michael

had a mean streak.

He could be vicious . . .

You got him upset, and

**he would cut
your heart out
to win.**

Doug Collins
Former Chicago Bulls Coach

DEFENSE
is
what
WINS
championships.

Michael Jordan

When **Michael** took over in the fourth quarter, it was like a shark in a feeding frenzy . . .

He *sensed the blood in the water and went for it.*

John Bach
Former Chicago Bulls Defensive Coach

I go out there and get my eyes **gouged,** *my nose* **busted,** *my body* **slammed.** *I love the* **pain** *of the game; it makes me feel* **alive.**

I've
always loved
pain . . .
I'll go out there
with **blood**
running down
my jersey
or a bone
sticking out of
my arm,
and I'll still be
diving *for*
loose balls.

Dennis Rodman

Fueled by desire,

he creates moments of wizardry,

causing expressions of disbelief

from his opponents,

provoking screams of love and adulation

from his fans.

He stands alone . . .

with the gods.

Gerald Sprayregen

Michael leaves his heart and soul out there every night.

He plays when he's bruised and banged up, he never wants to come out of the game for a rest.

He's from the old, hard-nosed school of basketball.

Doug Collins
Former Chicago Bulls Coach

Wes Unseld used to tell
his Washington Bullets

"Nail him"

on every drive.

John Starks scratched

and clawed

and left me scarred

for life.

Michael Jordan

I concentrate

on knocking in

the shot.

If I thought

of the number

of people

who were watching me

as I got ready to shoot,

I'd miss it.

I'm serious—

I would be unable

to make it.

Michael Jordan

He is a warrior,

a smiling warrior to be sure. . . .

Great athletes are not necessarily

nice people,

in the traditional definition of nice,

which implies a certain balanced, relaxed attitude

toward life.

They are, at least in their youth, **obsessed by winning**

by conquering others.

David Halberstam

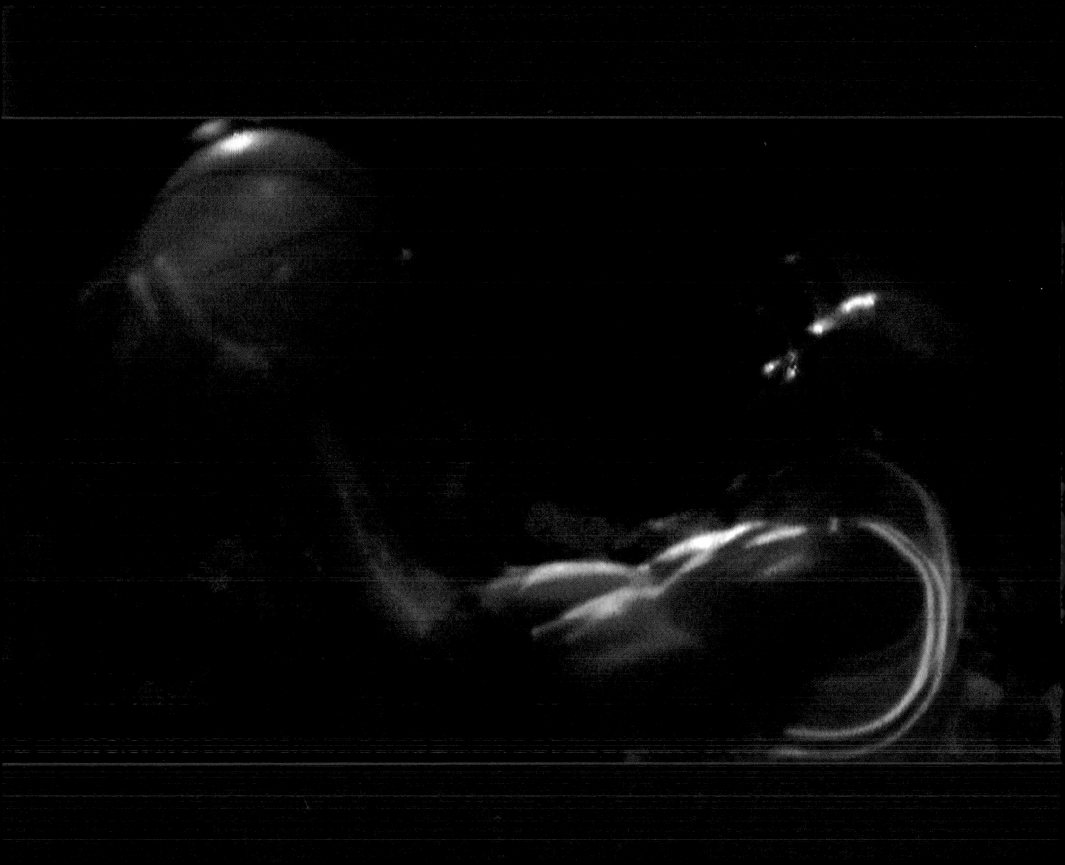

The curtain has been lifted and finally the Michael and Scottie show has begun.

Although the script will be left to their improvisation, the ultimate outcome has been preordained, and even their bravado-filled foes have already read tomorrow's headlines.

Gerald Sprayregen

Toni's my project.

I have the chance

to get him

to understand

basketball

is simple.

He makes it

too complicated.

There's a lot of

potential there . . .

it's simple.

Just play.

Toni Kukoc

Michael Jordan

Can you guard me?

Can you stop this?

I'm going this way, are you with me?

I just wanted to get inside their head.

I would be playing against a rookie,

and I might say,

"You watch me on TV,

you can change the channel;

you can't now." . . .

But if I could put some kind of doubt

in their mind then I had an advantage.

Michael Jordan

I *think* Michael *was one of the most*

feared defenders in the league . . .

The first time we played Orlando,

he went and blocked

a couple of Shaquille O'Neal's shots

at the beginning of the game.

That changed O'Neal's way of thinking

for the rest of the game.

That's just one way he could

change a game with just his defense.

Phil Jackson, Former Chicago Bulls Coach

He *tugs on their shorts, he laughs,*
a snide remark, a joke,
a thoroughly thought-out
glance of disdain,

all orchestrated to allow MJ
that half-second advantage,
more than enough time
to secure inside position.

Gerald Sprayregen

The powerful forearm

is planted in the small

of **Pippen's back**,

attempting to halt the momentum of one of

the **Bulls' superstars.**

Outlaw's elbow now finds

the shoulder blade.

Suddenly, **Pippen** fakes left,

whirls right, and finishes the play

with a left-handed slam-dunk.

Gerald Sprayregen

Me? A coach? . . .

I could never imagine myself
coaching in the NBA.
Now here it was—a reality. . . .
Coaching seemed like an impossible
profession:
watching, critiquing,
dealing with egocentric players like me. . . .

Was I ready for this?

Phil Jackson, Former Chicago Bulls Coach

When **I**
started working
for the **Bulls,**
nobody was
more excited
than my son, **Ben.**
He worshipped
Michael Jordan.
Ben's dream was
to meet his hero
in the flesh. . . .

*They met
at a practice
and when
the excitement
wore off,*
Ben *became confused . . .*
**"What do I
have left?" he said,
"I've already achieved
my life's goal."**

Phil Jackson
Former Chicago Bulls Coach

Please
don't overlook me . . .

I'd like a chance.
I was young, and I was new,
and I would hear about how great
BIRD and MAGIC were,
and the voice inside of me
was saying,
"What makes them great
and not me?"
But now . . .
I think I've earned the right
not to hear their voices
anymore.

Michael Jordan

Michael Jordan is

*the greatest competitor
in the history of sports,
not just basketball.
This guy is an assassin
in shorts.*

Jack Ramsay
Hall of Fame Coach

The best defenders in the game
are Pippen and Jordan . . .
they're just so tough.

In each
playoff series,
they take away
one more thing
from the opponent
and then they're left standing
out there naked,
without a stitch
of clothes.
It's embarrassing.

Jack Ramsay
Hall of Fame Coach

Michael

*will be
remembered
as the
greatest player
ever.*

just want to be
remembered
as a
great player,
period.

Scottie Pippen

In the final two minutes of a close game,
we often put him against the opposition's best scorer,
regardless of size or position,
and it was just awesome to watch
Michael *go to work . . .*

He was like a Tasmanian Devil

like all the furies of hell unleashed.

John Bach
Former Chicago Bulls Defensive Coach

*They're very
special people,*
those DINOSAURS,
those
ELEPHANTS,
those
RHINOCEROSES.
*Whatever
you want to call
those*
BIG BODIES
*out there,
they're of a
special value
in this league.*

Phil Jackson
Former Chicago Bulls Coach

Luc Longley

He made sport
into art

in a way that we really
haven't seen,
haven't admired, quite so,
since the Greeks
chose athletes,
foremost, to decorate
their amphoras.

In the end,
whenever the end,
it wasn't so much
the basketball.
It was the beauty.
It truly was a thing of
beauty.

Frank DeFord

When it's played the way it's spozed to be played,

**basketball happens in the air,
the pure air;**

flying, floating, elevated above the floor,

levitating the way oppressed peoples of this earth

imagine themselves in their dreams. . . .

As we envision soaring and swooping, extending,

refining the combat zone of basketball

into a fourth, outer, other dimension,

the dream ozone of flight without wings,

it's **Michael Jordan** we must recognize

as the truest prophet

of what might be possible.

John Edgar Wideman

*His defiant steel eyes are locked in mortal combat
with the will of the invading offensive machine.
Each is an intimidator, one because of his size,
the other because of his reputation.*

In a second, their minds and bodies will clash, but now they are momentarily frozen, awaiting their own instinctive reactions.

Gerald Sprayregen

*Somewhere about the middle of training camp, I realized I was having a lot of fun coaching this team and **Dennis Rodman**. He brings a lot of levity to the game. I mean I get a kick out of watching him play. . . . He reminds me of me.*

Phil Jackson
Former Chicago Bulls Coach

If

I *can reach the*

aggressiveness

of these guys,

MJ and Pippen,

that will be the

best thing
I ever did

in basketball as
a **personal goal.**

Toni Kukoc

There are

some players

who are

unique,

who

transcend

every aspect

of the game.

No one in the history

of the game

has had the impact

he has.

Pat Riley
Miami Heat Coach

He *could be the* **best defensive player** *ever.*

Karl Malone, Utah Jazz,
speaking about Scottie Pippen

*E*very time I play, I feel like I've got something to prove.

Getting cut in high school has a lot to do with that . . .

I know it's years later, but I still refuse to take anything for granted.

I GET UP FOR EVERY GAME.

I NEED THAT KIND OF INTENSITY.

THAT'S WHAT KEEPS ME GOING.

The

basketball court

for me, during a game,

is the most

peaceful place

I can imagine.

I truly feel

less pressure there

than any place

I go . . .

I

worry

about

nothing.

Being

out there

is one of

the

most

private parts

of

my

life.

Michael Jordan

I've met a number of players
who think they could be
(or are) as talented as
Michael Jordan,
but believe me, they have neither
MJ's fortitude nor his commitment.
No matter whether it's golf,
basketball, or . . .
MJ gives it his all.
In all my years, I have never seen
an athlete as revered as **MJ.**
*H*e is idolized by everyone,
friend and foe alike.

Wilt Chamberlain

I never had a real problem
getting along with my coaches.
Loughery helped me learn about being a pro . . .
Doug helped me reach the height of my potential

as a player,

and Phil created a situation for winning

championships.

But sometimes it seemed like Phil

wanted me to give up a few shots

and a few points for the sake of the team.

That was hard because it seemed like

it would hurt our chances to win.

But he probably had a different

point of view.

Michael Jordan

Steve Kerr

They come, and they go—one year, two years, more if they are lucky.

They are called the supporting cast, JORDANAIRS,

TEAMMATES, MICHAEL AND HIS DISCIPLES,

In basketball lingo, they are called JOURNEYMEN.

Randy Brown

Scott Burrell

They enjoy brief moments of heroics, but are always overshadowed by "THE MAN."

When they move on, they carry with them stories for a lifetime,

and a $5,000 symbol that proves that once they were part of history,

part of a team that won the NBA Championship.

I can dictate what I want to do
in the course of a game.

I can say to my friends,

Well, I'll score 12 points in the first quarter . . .

then I can relax in the second quarter

and score maybe six, eight . . . not take as many shots,

but in the second half I can go 15, 16, quick.

That's how much confidence I have
in my ability to dictate
how many points I can score.

Michael Jordan

Jordan *knew that if he were to wave,*

or even gesture,

the opening would be gone.

So he did it with his eyes and his mouth;

he tried to will his teammate

into seeing him by the strength

of the passion in his eyes

and the silent plea on his face.

Bob Greene

In the public eye,
everybody wants to be
the all-American hero.
There was always
this feeling that
success came about
because we had Michael....

I was able to step
out of Michael's shadow
and receive some things, endorsements.
But did we ever get
the justice just by us
having success?

Scottie Pippen

*Everybody says there's **me and Larry**. Really, there's **Michael** and there's everybody else. **Michael** was the most exciting out of all of us. . . . He could do the impossible and unbelievable . . .*

Larry and I

could never score

two points and

leave the crowd

going crazy like

it was the greatest move

you ever saw.

We couldn't leave you

with your mouth

hanging open

like **Michael**

could.

Magic Johnson
Basketball Hall of Famer

Ron
is the unsung hero of this team.

Scottie Pippen

*Some nights it's **red** . . .*
*some nights it's **green** . . .*
*some nights it's **multi-colored** . . .*
*but tonight, it's **blond**.*

Perhaps he's crazy, perhaps he's smart like a fox,
perhaps it doesn't matter.

What he does on a basketball court,
he does brilliantly.

You can buy

a ticket

and you can buy

a cap

with the

logo of your

favorite team,

but never fool

yourself

into thinking that

you're

one of them.

You
aren't.

It's their

special club out

there,

and none

of us

could

ever hope

to be

a member

of it.

Bob Greene

[Guarding] Jordan is like a
nightmare.

I have dreams about it.

Especially when the tongue comes out.

When the tongue comes out,

he's going to the rack.

Craig Ehlo
Seattle Super-Sonics Player

An off-day during the middle of the 1993 season.

In less-troubled times, shopping at the mall was at least possible.

But after five or six years in the league,

it turned into a situation where

there had to be a significant purpose for me to leave the house.

Forget running to the 7-11 for a quart of milk.

Stealing early-morning breakfasts in a corner booth at Baker's Square

or imposing on understanding downtown Chicago restaurant owners

for late-night dinners became so tiring

that eating out meant building my own restaurant.

Michael Jordan

I'm feeling
like an old guy,

if you want to know the truth.

Not that I don't still have

the enthusiasm to do the job.

I do. But I'm wiser now.

'm preparing for the end.
The end of my life
in basketball.

The hungry young kid is still inside me,

and I can find him when I need him,

but these days it's mostly

the wise old guy
who I find.

Michael Jordan

How do I tell a man
I got love for **good-bye**,
*when I really don't
want him to leave . . .
a man that I really
don't know very well,
but who has been
a very significant part
of my life. . . .*
**I can't kiss him,
hug him,**
give him a pound.
[He] *made my love for a game
I already worshipped
unconditional.
How do I tell this man*
good-bye?

Scoop Jackson

I still want to win championships.

Those championships keep me feeling the love for the game.

I just can't wait

for the

PLAYOFFS

to start.

The

CHAMPIONSHIPS

now

are the only reason

I'm playing.

Michael Jordan

There's still a

burning flame

in here.

The best there ever was. The best there ever will be.

Michael Jordan Statue, United Center, Chicago